PHEASANT HUNTING

by Tom Carpenter

Content Consultant
Bill Sherck
Outdoor Television Show Host

SportsZone

An Imprint of Abdo Publishing
abdopublishing.com

abdopublishing.com

Published by Abdo Publishing, a division of ABDO, PO Box 398166, Minneapolis, Minnesota 55439. Copyright © 2016 by Abdo Consulting Group, Inc. International copyrights reserved in all countries. No part of this book may be reproduced in any form without written permission from the publisher. SportsZone™ is a trademark and logo of Abdo Publishing.

Printed in the United States of America, North Mankato, Minnesota
042015
092015

Cover Photos: Joy Stein/Shutterstock Images (background); Tom Reichner/Shutterstock Images (foreground)
Interior Photos: Joy Stein/Shutterstock Images, 1 (background); Tom Reichner/Shutterstock Images, 1 (foreground); iStockphoto, 4–5, 20–21, 27, 37, 38; Lezlie Sterling/Sacramento Bee/MCT/Newscom, 6, 8; Adam Fichna/Shutterstock Images, 12–13; Jörn Friederich/Image Broker/Newscom, 15; Usher, D./Picture Alliance/Arco Images G/Newscom, 16; Michael Pearce/The Wichita Eagle/AP Images, 18; Steven Hausler/Hays Daily News/AP Images, 23; Matt Stauss/iStockphoto, 24; Shutterstock Images, 30–31; Brent Frazee/Kansas City Star/TNS/Newscom, 32; Steven Oehlenschlager/Dreamstime, 34–35; Fred Hunt/Hays Daily News/AP Images, 40–41; Brad Nading/Garden City Telegram/AP Images, 42; Dale Spartas/Corbis, 44

Editor: Jon Westmark
Series Designer: Jake Nordby

Library of Congress Control Number: 2015931756

Cataloging-in-Publication Data
Carpenter, Tom.
 Pheasant hunting / Tom Carpenter.
  p. cm. -- (Hunting)
Includes bibliographical references and index.
ISBN 978-1-62403-835-8
1. Pheasant shooting--Juvenile literature.   I. Title.
799.2/4627--dc23

                                                    2015931756

CONTENTS

Chapter 1

WELCOME TO PHEASANT HUNTING

A girl and her parents step out of a farmhouse. The air is crisp but starting to warm as the morning sun moves higher in the sky. A young dog bounds around the trio. It is a German

Pheasants are often out feeding when the sun comes up.

shorthaired pointer, and its high energy level and great sense of smell make it a good hunting dog. This morning it will help the family hunt ring-necked pheasants.

Pointing dogs freeze in place to let hunters know when there is a bird nearby.

At the end of the barnyard, the hunters stop to load their shotguns. They enter a harvested wheat field, spread into a line, and begin to walk slowly along. Their dog runs back and forth in front of them, searching for the scent of birds.

When the hunters are approximately halfway through the field of prairie grass, a couple of pheasants flush. The birds are too far away to shoot at. Pheasants are careful and alert birds. This makes them tough to bag.

The hunters keep going. Soon the dog is working harder. Its sniffs the ground and wags its tail excitedly. Then the dog stands still. Its nose is pointed down, and its stubby tail is locked straight out. Its nostrils quiver. The dog is pointing. It has been bred and trained to do this. Pointing usually means a pheasant is hiding nearby.

The mother calls the girl over. The young hunter quietly walks in from the side, trying to flush the pheasant that is somewhere ahead of the dog.

Dogs help hunters quickly track down and retrieve their pheasants.

Kyak-kyak-kyak-kyak! A male ringneck, or rooster, cackles and launches itself up from the grass. The pheasant is loud, colorful, and bigger than a chicken! It startles the young hunter. But she has practiced hard with her shotgun. She stays focused.

She brings the shotgun up and swings it toward the bird in one smooth motion. By now the bird is nearly 30 yards (27 m) out. *Boom!* The pheasant tumbles through the air to the ground. The dog runs over, digs around in the wheat stalks, and hurries back with a colorful ringneck in its mouth.

The family takes a break from hunting to admire the bird. It is a male, called a rooster or cock. It has a red eye patch, a green and purple head, and a white ring around its neck. It has bronze and powder blue feathers on its body and long tail feathers. The legs have long, sharp spurs. The bird is a trophy to be proud of.

Pheasant Hunting History

Ring-necked pheasants are not native to the United States. They are native to China and the Korean peninsula. Pheasants were introduced successfully in North America for the first time in 1881 in Oregon's Willamette Valley. America's landscape was changing at this time. Large areas of wilderness grassland were being turned into farmland. Native game birds, such as prairie chickens, were not adapting well to the changes. But the new habitat was perfect for pheasants.

Game departments and sportsmen's clubs began introducing pheasants in other states. By the early 1900s, pheasants were in many states across the Midwest.

Pheasant populations have gone up and down many times since their territory expanded. Their numbers depend on how much habitat is available. They need cover so that they can nest, raise their young, and hide from predators and winter weather.

Today pheasants are important game birds that are symbols of a healthy landscape. Ringnecks offer an exciting hunt in the beautiful farmlands of the US heartland.

Pheasant Range

Since being introduced in Oregon in 1881, pheasants have found good habitats across North America.

Chapter 2

BIOLOGY AND HABITAT

Successful pheasant hunters understand ringnecks' habitats and habits. Doing so helps hunters find more birds and get more shots.

Male pheasants' bright colors help them attract mates.

Physical Traits

A full-grown rooster weighs 2 1/2 to 3 pounds
(1.1–1.4 kg). It measures 30 to 36 inches
(76–91 cm) from the tip of its beak to the end of

its long tail. The tail itself can be longer than 20 inches (51 cm).

Female ring-necked pheasants are called hens. Hens are not as brightly colored as roosters. Their feathers are speckled with browns, tans, and creams that make great camouflage. They have black eyes. Mature hens weigh from 1 3/4 to 2 1/4 pounds (0.8–1 kg). They measure from 21 to 25 inches (53–64 cm) in length. Hens' tails are usually no longer than 12 inches (30 cm).

Surviving Winter

Pheasants struggle against winter weather. If deep snow covers their food, pheasants cannot get enough to eat. If the birds have a lot of fat on their bodies going into winter, they may be able to survive without much food. But they still need thick cover to protect against strong, cold winds. Sometimes pheasants tunnel into snowbanks to insulate themselves from the cold outside. This also hides the birds from predators.

Behavior

Despite their colors, rooster pheasants are good at hiding from predators. The birds are extremely cautious. They have

Pheasants are masters at using tall or thick grass to stay out of sight.

excellent hearing and eyesight. They prefer to run, rather than fly, at the first sound or sight of danger. They can run as fast as 10 miles per hour (16 km/h). The birds will keep running and then flush when they think they are away from danger.

Pheasant chicks immediately leave the nest with the hen in search for food.

Hens are equally careful. But their dull colors make them better at hiding in grasses. This helps them safely nest and raise their young.

Breeding and Nesting

Pheasants breed in spring. Roosters fight over hens. The cocks kick one another with the sharp spurs on their legs. The winning roosters strut about, flapping their wings and cackling loudly to attract hens.

Hens lay six to 15 eggs in nests hidden in tall grass. The eggs are an olive green color. They hatch after approximately 25 days. The chicks follow the hen for six or seven weeks. The young pheasants learn how to find food and escape predators.

Nesting Needs

To nest successfully, ring-necked pheasants need grasslands. The birds nest in spring before the new year's grass has grown tall. So they need grass that is still standing from the previous summer and fall. It is important that this grass does not get mowed. Otherwise pheasant nests would be destroyed. If pheasants have good grass for nesting and raising chicks, populations can grow quickly. Heavy rains can make very young chicks cold and wet. This can kill them. Dry weather helps pheasants nest successfully.

Some hunters choose to walk fields without dogs. These hunters walk in a zigzag pattern to scare up birds.

Habitat

The best pheasant habitat is a mix of grain fields, wetlands, and thickets. Thick forest edges, grassy roadside ditches, and fence lines full of brush are also good pheasant habitats.

Pheasants sleep at night tucked under heavy grass cover. In the early morning, the birds go to open areas, such as hayfields and harvested grain fields, to feed. By midmorning pheasants head into thick grass, brush, cattails, or other cover to spend the day. Late in the afternoon, the birds head out to feeding areas again. At sunset, pheasants walk, run, or fly to roosting grass again for the night.

Pheasants eat a variety of foods. In summer the birds eat insects, seeds, and tender green leaves from plants. In late summer and autumn, pheasants love to eat grain left over in harvested fields of corn, wheat, oats, milo, barley, and soybeans.

Chapter 3

TECHNIQUES

In many kinds of hunting, hunters wait for game
to come to them. Pheasant hunting is different.
In pheasant hunting, the hunter walks, often
with a dog, in search of birds. The goal is to

Hunters must be ready to aim and shoot when they walk through pheasant habitat.

flush pheasants into the air and take a shot. Only roosters are legal game in pheasant hunting. This gives hens a chance to survive the winter and raise chicks in the spring.

Pheasant hunters do not just wander the countryside. Successful pheasant hunters understand ringneck habits and use smart techniques. These hunters stay quiet. They work well with their dogs and with other hunters.

Hunting Grounds

The first step to successful pheasant hunting is recognizing places that may hold birds. The best pheasant hunting happens in areas where cover and crops meet. These are called transition zones. A harvested grain field next to grassy cover is ideal. So are areas where wetlands meet grasslands or harvested crop fields. On bad-weather days, pheasants tend to be in thicker cover. On sunny days, the birds tend to be in thinner cover.

Stealth Hunting Approaches

Inexperienced pheasant hunters often make a big mistake. They don't respect the ringneck's keen hearing and eyesight.

Many hunters walk near the edges of fields to cover multiple habitats.

Pheasant hunting starts as soon as the hunters arrive in the area where they plan to hunt. If they arrive in a vehicle, hunters should not slam their car doors. They should avoid talking or laughing loudly. As they hunt, good hunters continue to be quiet. They whisper instead of yelling back and forth. It is best to surprise pheasants. That might get the birds to flush!

Well-trained hunting dogs can respond to whistle or voice commands.

Many hunters use dogs to hunt pheasants. Dogs must also be stealthy. Running wildly through the hunting area can easily scare birds away before the hunter is close enough for a shot. Good hunters learn to direct their dogs through light toots on a whistle rather than by shouting. Hunters can communicate with their human hunting partners through hand signals. Hunters who do not stay quiet and stealthy often do not see pheasants. The birds run off or fly away.

Pheasant Hunting Strategies

Hunters cannot control the wind. But they can plan their hunt to keep the wind in their favor. Smart hunters try to walk into the wind as much as possible. This helps keep sounds they make from traveling too far ahead. It also gives hunting dogs a better chance to smell the birds.

It is good to pause often while pheasant hunting. Good hunters stop randomly for a few moments. This helps make any nearby pheasants nervous. It is also smart to zigzag through the cover. This keeps birds guessing where the hunter will go next. Zigzagging is best for people hunting alone or in pairs. Zigzagging is hard for big groups to coordinate.

One good pheasant hunting strategy is to go back through areas that have already been hunted. Ringnecks can be sneaky. They will often hide and stay put, letting hunters pass by. Coming back toward the birds from a new angle can get them to flush.

The best ringneck hunters always walk with their shotgun ready. Pheasants flush quickly and fly away fast. Hunters who are ready to shoot will bag more birds.

Hunting with Dogs

Pheasant hunters use two types of dogs—flushers and pointers.

Flushers, or flushing dogs, work within 20 to 30 yards (18 to 27 m) of the hunters. This is within shooting range. These dogs run back and forth in front of the hunter and look for birds. When the dog smells a pheasant, it chases the bird and flushes it into the air.

Hunters can tell when flushers are following birds. The dogs get excited and wag their tails faster than usual. Good flushing dog breeds include Labrador retrievers, golden retrievers, and springer spaniels.

Flushers, such as Labrador retrievers, are great at forcing birds to jump into the air.

Pointing dogs often work a little farther from the hunter than flushing dogs do. The pointer's job is to find a bird and then lock into a point. This means the dog stands perfectly still with its nose toward the bird. Then the hunter walks in the direction the dog points in order to flush the bird. Good pointing dog breeds for pheasant hunting include Brittanys, English setters, and German shorthaired pointers.

Hunting in Groups

Sometimes hunters get together in groups and hunt pheasants together. It is smart to post hunters at the end of the hunting area. These people are called blockers. They surprise birds running ahead of the line of hunters. The hunters space themselves across the cover, usually about 10 to 20 yards (9–18 m) apart. Without blockers the birds may run ahead of the other hunters and fly away out of shooting range.

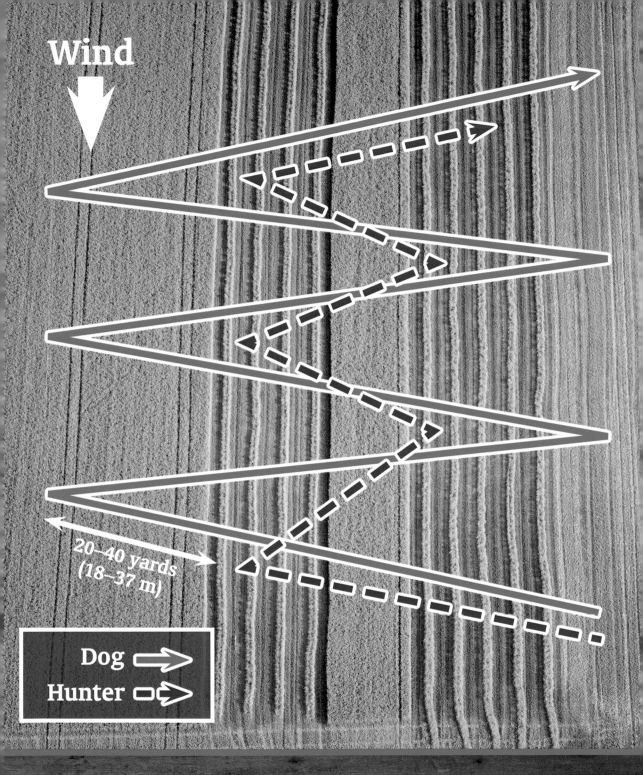

Wind

20–40 yards
(18–37 m)

Dog ⇨
Hunter ⊏⇨

Zigzagging with a dog can help a hunter cover lots of ground. Once the dog goes far enough one way, the hunter can command it to change direction.

Chapter 4

EQUIPMENT AND SKILLS

To bag roosters consistently, pheasant hunters must use the right equipment and accessories. They must also master several important skills, including scouting and quick and accurate shooting.

Hunters must learn how to handle their shotguns effectively in order to be safe and successful.

Pheasant Hunting Equipment

Firearms are the most important piece of equipment for hunters. Pheasant hunters use shotguns. Shotguns are loaded with shells that shoot pellets—also called shot or BBs—out of

Blaze orange hats and vests help pheasant hunters stay safe when hunting together.

the barrel. The pellets spread out downrange. This raises the likelihood of hitting and bringing down flying birds.

Hunters like to use shells, or loads, with a lot of gunpowder and large pellets. Pheasants can be tough. Bigger pellets deliver more force to bring the birds down.

Pheasant hunters do a lot of walking when looking for birds. Comfortable, sturdy boots are important. Sturdy but light boots are good in mild weather. If the weather is cold or there is snow on the ground, comfortable pac boots with insulation inserts are good.

Some pheasant habitat is wet. In this case, hunters should wear waterproof boots to keep their feet dry and warm.

Pheasant hunting does not require a lot of special clothing. It is nice to have brush pants to protect the legs. These are special jeans with reinforced fronts that fend off briars, thorns, and burrs. Pheasant hunters often wear jackets or vests with game pouches to carry birds they have shot. Most states require hunters to wear some blaze orange clothing. This helps pheasant hunters see one another.

Dog Accessories

Dogs also need hunting supplies. Hunters should carry water for their dogs to drink. Most hunters carry a whistle to communicate with and instruct their dogs. Some also use electronic beeper collars that help track their dogs. It is smart to carry tweezers to pull out any thorns the dog may get in its paws. Some hunters carry a light first-aid kit made for dogs.

Shotgun: Shotguns allow hunters to cover larger areas with their shots.

Water: Water helps hunters and dogs stay hydrated and energetic throughout the hunt.

Game Pouch: Game pouches store game so that hunters can keep their hands free.

PHEASANT HUNTING EQUIPMENT

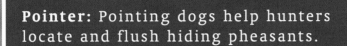

Pointer: Pointing dogs help hunters locate and flush hiding pheasants.

Electronic Collar: Electronic collars beep to let hunters keep track of their dogs and know when the dogs are pointing.

It is a good idea to dress in layers of thin clothing for pheasant hunting. Doing this allows hunters to remove layers to stay cool. It can be easy to overheat while walking, even on cold days. Warm gloves are important in cold weather. But gloves should also allow hunters to operate their shotguns effectively.

Pheasant Hunting Skills

Scouting often pays off for pheasant hunters. Driving down back roads early in the morning and in the evening are good ways to spot pheasants and locate areas to hunt.

After hunters locate good pheasant habitat, they need to make sure it is legal to hunt in the area. Pheasant hunters sometimes hunt on public land. Other times state game agencies lease private land for public hunting. State game department websites identify lands open to the public and help hunters find them.

But many pheasants live on private land. Hunters need to get permission from the landowner to hunt in these

Pheasant hunters often need to gain permission to hunt in fields they do not own.

areas. The best approach is to meet with the owner before hunting season starts and ask politely to use the land. Many landowners appreciate this approach and give the hunter permission to use their land.

Once hunters have land to hunt on, they must be ready to make the most of their opportunities. To do this, hunters must be able to make their shots.

Many hunters practice their aim by shooting at flying
clay targets at firing ranges.

Pheasants often flush without warning and fly fast.

Good shooters bring the gun up to their shoulder steadily

and confidently. They track the bird while looking down the

barrel. They swing the barrel past the bird, aiming in front of it. Then they pull the trigger. If the hunter aims directly at the bird, the bird will have moved by the time the pellets arrive. Aiming in front of the bird is called leading the shot.

Pheasants have long tails. Shooting at a pheasant's body will likely result in a hit to the tail. The best shooters attempt to hit the bird's head and neck. Most hunters practice shooting at moving targets before the season begins. This helps ensure they will be ready to bag a bird when the time comes.

Searching for downed birds without a dog can be difficult. It is important to note where the bird went down and move to that place as quickly and safely as possible. After locating the bird, it is important to field dress it. This helps cool the meat and keep it from going bad. Timely field dressing assures great taste later. It is also illegal in most states to waste meat.

Chapter 5

SAFETY AND CONSERVATION

As with all kinds of hunting, pheasant hunters
must follow firearm safety rules. All hunters
should take a firearm safety course to learn
how to handle their guns safely and effectively.

When hunting in groups, pheasant hunters must pay special attention to shooting safety. Groups should discuss the rules before the hunt. Hunters walking in a line across a field should only shoot in front of or behind the line and high

Pheasant hunters should shoot only at birds higher than human height.

into the air. They should never shoot to the side or at pheasants flying low. Either of those shots could hit other hunters.

Hunters who are blocking at the end of a field follow similar rules. They shoot only at birds flying high in the air so they do not hit people. They avoid shooting toward other blockers.

Most states require hunters to wear blaze orange hats and some blaze orange clothing. This helps hunters keep track of each other and not shoot in one another's direction.

Licensing and Conservation

Pheasant hunters must hold the appropriate hunting license for the state in which they are hunting. Many states also require ringneck hunters to have a Pheasant Stamp. Money from the purchase of Pheasant Stamps goes to conservation efforts. Conservation is the wise use of natural resources. Conservation is important to pheasant hunting because it helps protect ringneck habitat. This keeps pheasant populations up. Hunters must stick their Pheasant Stamps to their licenses and sign both so that only they can use them.

TAB-K Formula

One good way to remember how to be safe with a firearm is by following the TAB-K formula:

T— Treat every firearm as if it were loaded at all times.

A— Always point the barrel of the gun in a safe direction.

B— Be certain of your target and what's beyond it.

K— Keep your finger outside of the trigger guard until you are ready to shoot.

Responsible pheasant hunting is a fun way to enjoy nature and provide meat for the family.

Pheasant hunters are usually limited to shooting roosters. This leaves more hens for nesting in the spring. Bag limits vary by state, so pheasant hunters should study hunting regulations carefully. In some states, bag limits increase midway through the season, when fewer people are pheasant hunting.

To support conservation, many pheasant hunters join organizations such as Pheasants Forever. Pheasants Forever works to conserve and set aside habitat across ringneck range. Ducks Unlimited also does work that benefits pheasant habitat.

Ring-necked pheasants do best where there is a good mix of cover and crop fields as habitat. Grasslands, grain fields, wild prairie, wetlands, and brushy tangles create a habitat that can support high pheasant populations for hunters to enjoy on the best autumn days.

GLOSSARY

bag limit
The number of pheasants a hunter can legally shoot in one day.

briars
Prickly seed pods that stick to hunters' clothing and dogs' hair.

flush
When a bird jumps off the ground and flies away.

lease
An agreement between a game department and a landowner to allow public hunting on the landowner's land.

load
The combination of pellets and gunpowder that makes up a shotgun shell.

native
Originating from a particular place.

pac boots
Boots made from waterproofed rubber and leather, often with a liner made of felt or wool.

shotgun
A firearm that shoots a shell loaded with pellets. The pellets spread out in the air, offering a better chance to hit flying game.

spurs
Sharp, pointed extensions on a rooster pheasant's lower leg.

FOR MORE INFORMATION

Further Reading

Furstinger, Nancy. *Pointers*. Minneapolis: Abdo Publishing, 2006.

Llanas, Sheila Griffin. *Common Pheasant*. Minneapolis: Abdo Publishing, 2014.

Pound, Blake. *Pheasant Hunting*. Minneapolis: Bellwether Media, Inc., 2013.

Websites

To learn more about Hunting, visit **booklinks.abdopublishing.com**. These links are routinely monitored and updated to provide the most current information available.

INDEX

ABOUT THE AUTHOR

Tom Carpenter is a father, a sportsman, and an outdoor writer. He has introduced many children, including his three sons, to the thrills and rewards of hunting. A native son of Wisconsin who always has part of his heart in South Dakota, he planted roots in the middle. He lives with his family near the shores of Bass Lake, Minnesota.